MW01204758

North Korean Keys to Revival

LESSONS FROM THE JERUSALEM OF THE EAST

DANIEL M. WEAVER

This is the 2nd edition of a book formerly published in 2017 under the title: Pyongyang Revival, Will the Holy Spirit visit again?

<u>Acknowledgements</u>

Many thanks to my friend Dr. Everett Wade for his topical insight and editing assistance.

Lasting thanks to my mother for her patience as I struggled to learn how to express thoughts in the written form during years of homeschooling.

Special thanks to my wife for enduring many hours of my divided attention as I was preoccupied with this project.

Complete thanks to my Lord, without whose help and guidance this would never have been possible. May He take the small fish and loaves offered here and multiply greatly.

Cover design by You-Young Kim
https://youyoungkim.com/

Revival Publishing
Memphis, TN

ISBN: 0-9989406-1-5
ISBN-13: 978-0-9989406-1-8

Table of Contents

Editorial Note

Much of this book is not original to the author, but was compiled from multiple sources. These sources have been combined and some quotations have been edited for clarity. The author has added transitions between the source materials and attempted to draw out lessons relevant to our current situation. For further understanding of the Korean revival, the author encourages the reader to return to the original accounts. These sources are listed in the back of the book for further reading.

For additional information regarding this revival and a free bonus story on the Khassia Hills revival which preceded the Pyongyang revival, visit:

https://danielmweaver.com/northkoreankeystorevival

Introduction

Christians who live in the United States of America seem to have forgotten that the words in the Bible are not theories, but are directions from God on how to conduct their life. The high concepts of sin, grace, love, and judgment—and the insight into the mysteries of the spiritual beings we call God and His angels—are not set down on paper for us to contemplate only on Sunday mornings, nor are they merely recorded for the dedicated to study and expound to others. Though there is now such a thing as a Christian religion, the followers of "the Way" in the first century were willing to suffer and die, not because they were attracted to a new and novel alternative religion, but because they were influenced by and submitted to the living Christ Jesus, who turned the known world upside down even after being killed and buried.

This Jesus, who died on a Roman cross, was speaking to and through the believers, and the church was not yet an organization, but rather a gathering of those whose lives had been changed by believing on the Lord Jesus Christ. The Bible was not study material to be debated, picked through for moral truths, then discarded as impractical and applicable only to someone else, but was recognized as "God-breathed" (2 Tim 3:16 NIV) and the very place one could turn to receive relevant personal instruction from God.

The original followers of Jesus are not historically unique in their dedication to Christ, but they set an example for many in subsequent centuries to be shining examples of those who let Christ reign over their lives, words and actions. Unfortunately, as time passed, knowledge of "the Way" became institutionalized as a religion. The Church lost the reality of each member being a functioning member of the body of Christ, as some were appointed as clergy to paid organizational positions, while the rest became the laity. Worship became a ceremony to be performed at set weekly times, rather than a spiritual sacrifice made daily by believers subjecting their lives to the living God.

These organizational rules and procedures allowed for some to satisfy the outward requirements of Church membership while showing little reality of a relationship with the risen Messiah. Those actually willing to conduct their lives according to the life of Christ became the exception rather than the rule even among those who professed to believe in Jesus as the salvation of mankind. Though these set-apart ones often have a lonely path to walk, there have been some notable exceptions in history when large groups were changed by encountering Christ's powerful risen life. In these instances, groups of people repented from a state of rebellion or apathy and turned to the Savior. The lives they lived afterward permanently reflected this encounter with the living God. We commonly refer to these large-scale movements of people turning to God as "revivals."[1]

Some revivals are widely known and studied, such as the Welsh revival. Another revival is not as well-known, overlooked by many Christians today despite its remarkable story. The revival I refer to is known as the Pyongyang Revival, which occurred in the city of Pyongyang, Korea in early 1907. The outcome of this revival could not be more dramatic, with the spread of the gospel across a formerly heathen nation having such impact that Pyongyang became known as the "Jerusalem of the East" due to its Christian character and gospel outreach. Within 50 years

---

[1] In some circles the term "revival" has been overused and may simply refer to annual special meetings which may or may not have any evidence of the Spirit's power. This book, however, uses "revival" to mean the Spirit coming in power upon a number of people within a short period of time with a resulting testimony of changed lives among those influenced.

after the revival, the country of Korea had been divided and Pyongyang is now known best as the capital of North Korea. This is an unfortunate eclipsing of the city's previous well-deserved reputation as a spiritual center for the entire region.

Though not well-known today, much was written about this revival as it occurred. The extreme expressions of conviction, confession, and repentance are thoroughly documented in books, newsletters, and written reports by missionaries close to the revival. These firsthand accounts are the basis of much of this book. The compilation here is not meant to replace the original writing, but rather to draw attention back to this tremendous move of the Spirit, while also proposing the Spirit will move again if we are but willing to do our part. Christians would do well to examine the Pyongyang Revival, not as a nostalgic glimpse into the past, but in order to identify what is lacking in the average Christian's current experience, and then to use these keys to prepare the way for another great move of God.

This writing will first explain the revival and its background, using firsthand accounts to maintain accuracy, and then set forth several key factors which enabled the Spirit to sweep across a land and transform a society. Notably lacking as a key factor is the presence of a central figure in the revival. The Pyongyang Revival was not the result of a powerful preacher or some tremendously spiritual individual, but rather the result of ordinary believers taking very practical steps to prepare the way for the Lord to give a blessing to His people.

The practical steps the believers took to prepare for the Pyongyang Revival are proposed in this book as keys to revival. The purpose, and the author's hope and prayer, is that this account would encourage readers to use these keys in their own lives to pave the way for another move of the Spirit, which is needed just as desperately today as it was in Korea in 1900.

Revival!

It is altogether improbable that religion will ever make progress among heathen nations except through the influence of revivals. The attempt is now being made to do it by education, and other cautious and gradual improvements. But so long as the laws of mind remain what they are, it cannot be done in this way. There must be excitement sufficient to wake up the dormant moral powers, and roll back the tide of degradation and sin.

- Charles Finney, 1835 [2]

"At every meeting the slain of the Lord are laid out all over the church and sometimes out in the yard. Men and women are stricken down and become unconscious under the power of conviction," wrote Rev. W. A. Noble from Pyongyang, Korea in February, 1907. He stated, "We are having the most wonderful

---

[2] (Finney, 1835)

manifestations of the outpouring of the Holy Spirit on the native church that I have ever seen or heard, perhaps there has been no greater demonstration of Divine power since the Apostles' days."[3]

The foreign missionaries had a sense of wonder at becoming active participants in a move of God that would effectively spread the good news of the gospel across the entire country of Korea in a few short years. In contrast to some countries where missionaries labored for decades with little visible fruit, Korea was like a flower which bloomed suddenly, in response to the morning light. As one account stated, "There has taken place in Korea the most sudden turning of a nation to God that has been witnessed in the world's history."[4]

---

[3] (Federal Council of Protestant Evangelical Missions in Korea, 1907)

[4] (Davis, 1910)

The first Protestant missionaries to settle in Korea arrived in 1887, providentially setting foot on shore on Easter Sunday. These first two missionaries were only allowed into Korea as medical professionals and professors offering practical help to a nation falling behind in technological advancement. After the groundwork and relationship building done by the initial two, other missionaries began to arrive in response to the call for help in meeting the great spiritual hunger of the Korean people, and many of the missionaries had been on the field for five years or less when the Spirit began to move in 1903.

From the beginning stages of the revival in Wonsan, it would be four years until the Spirit moved mightily in Pyongyang in 1907. When we compare this to work in China, India, or other mission fields that required decades of efforts before any significant outward results could be

Picture 1 - Memorial for one of the first protestant missionaries to set foot in Korea. Rev. Appenzeller was active in the translation work of the New Testament until a shipwreck in 1902 off the coast of Korea, in which he died while attempting to save a young Korean girl. This memorial is located at Yanghwajin Foreign Missionary Cemetery in Seoul, Korea. Photo by the author in September 2016.

seen, the amazement at the Pyongyang Revival starts to make more sense.

Jonathan Goforth, a Canadian missionary to China, visited Korea in 1907 gaining a firsthand look at the result and ongoing power of the revival. He later wrote a detailed account of the revival. This is how Goforth describes the lead up to the revival:

> Dr. Hardie, missionary to Gensan [also known as Wonsan], on the east coast of Korea, had been asked to prepare some addresses on prayer for a little conference the missionaries proposed to hold. As he was preparing his subjects, from John 14 and elsewhere, the Holy Spirit taught him many things. When he delivered his talks on prayer all the missionaries were moved. Afterward the Korean Christians met in conference and were very manifestly stirred. Dr. Hardie then visited ten mission centers throughout Korea

and gave his prayer talks, and during 1904, ten thousand Koreans turned to God. The revival thus begun continued in power and spiritual result until 1906.[5]

Dr. Lillias Horton Underwood, a medical doctor who had been in Korea as a missionary since the 1880s, adds vivid details:

> There continued to be isolated incidents of the Spirit moving, such as when Mr. Gerdine held services in Mokpo in October, 1906, twice a day for a week. The report came, saying: "The word was like a scalpel, laying bare the secret sins and hidden cancers of the soul. Strong men wept like children, confessing their sins, and as they realized the Saviour's forgiveness and peace with God, their faces shone and the church rang with hymns of triumph. Men stood six deep

---

[5] (Goforth, 1943)

waiting to testify of blessing received, sins forgiven, differences healed, victory over self, and baptism of the Spirit. From the beginning the spirit of prayer, intercession and confession was poured out in a remarkable way."[6]

Goforth's account continues:

Those ministering in Pyongyang did not expect to see greater blessings in Korea than they had seen up to the middle of 1906. When one compares the results in Korea with those in China, Japan and elsewhere, the success, at least when measured by numbers converted, had already far exceeded anything in those lands. It was therefore natural to conclude God probably did not intend to grant greater blessings than had already been seen, but a new vision took hold in September, 1906, when Dr. Howard A.

---

[6] (Underwood, 1908)

Johnston, of New York visited Seoul. Dr. Johnston informed the missionaries of the revival in the Khassia Hills, India, where they had baptized 8,200 converts during the two year period of 1905-1906. The missionaries returned home to Pyongyang humbled. There were over twenty in the Methodist and Presbyterian Missions at Pyongyang. They decided to pray at the noon hour until greater blessing came, reasoning God was not a respecter of persons, and therefore He did not wish to give greater blessings in the Khassia Hills than in Pyongyang.[7]

After praying daily for about a month, a brother proposed to stop the prayer meeting, saying, "We have prayed about a month, and nothing unusual has come of it. We are spending a lot of time. I don't

---

[7] For a free download about the revival of Khassia Hills, visit:
https://danielmweaver.com/northkoreankeystorevival/

think we are justified. Let us go on with our work as usual, and each pray at home as we find it convenient." The proposal seemed plausible. However, the majority decided to continue the prayer meeting, believing the Lord would not deny Pyongyang what He had granted to Khassia.

Deciding to give more time to prayer instead of less, the meeting time changed from twelve to four o'clock; then those gathered were free to pray until suppertime if they wished. There was little else but prayer. If anyone had an encouraging item to relate, it was given as they continued in prayer. They prayed about four months, and they said the result was that all forgot about being Methodists and Presbyterians; they only realized that they were all one in the Lord Jesus Christ. That was true church union; it was brought about on the knees; it would last; it would glorify the Most High.

About that time Mr. Swallen, along with Mr. Blair, [two of the missionaries based out of Pyongyang], visited one of the country out-stations. While conducting the service in the usual way, many began weeping and confessing their sins. Mr. Swallen said he had never met with anything so strange, and he announced a hymn, hoping to check the wave of emotion which was sweeping over the audience. He tried several times, but in vain, and in awe he realized that Another was managing that meeting, and he got as far out of sight as possible. The next morning he and Mr. Blair returned to the city rejoicing, and told how God had come to the out-station. All praised God and believed that the time to favor Pyongyang was close at hand.[8]

---

[8] (Goforth, 1943)

Referring to Dr. Underwood's perspective sets the stage for the revival's climax:

> It had now come to the first week of January, 1907. The missionaries all expected God would significantly bless them during the week of universal prayer. The Central Church in Pyongyang was full of men every night. The meetings grew in power until Saturday, which was best day of the whole week.[9]

Rev. Graham Lee, another missionary, recounts what happened next:

> On Sunday morning, regular services were held in each of the city's churches, then Sunday evening everyone gathered again at the Central Church in a continuation of the union meetings. The missionaries expected great things from that Sunday evening meeting, but instead

---

[9] (Underwood, 1908)

of receiving a great blessing, they had a most peculiar experience. The meeting seemed dead and God's Spirit seemed to have departed. After an address and a few perfunctory testimonies which testified to nothing, everyone went home with heavy hearts, wondering where the trouble lay. During the meetings before there had been testimonies which had life in them and confessions of sin which were real and earnest, but Sunday night everything seemed blocked and the meeting a dead formal thing.[10]

This experience caused the missionaries to cry out to God for help at their noon meeting the following day. They then gathered for the evening service, and Rev. Lee tells of the incredible hours which followed:

---

[10] (Lee, 1907)

We went to that Monday evening service, not knowing what would happen, but praying all the time that God would hear and answer. When we reached the building, I think we all felt that something was coming. After a short address, we had audible prayer together, all the audience joining in, and this audible prayer, by the way, has been one of the features of these meetings. After the prayer, there were a few testimonies and then the leader announced a song, asking the audience to rise and stating that all those who wished to go home could do so, as we intended to stay until morning if there were men who wished to remain that long and confess their sins. A great many went, but between five and six hundred remained. These we gathered into one side of the building and then began a meeting, the like of which none of us had ever seen.

After prayer, confessions were called for, and immediately the Spirit of God seemed to descend on that audience. Man after man would rise, confess his sins, break down and weep, and then throw himself to the floor and beat the floor with his fists in a perfect agony of conviction. My own cook tried to make a confession, broke down in the midst of it, and cried to me across the room, "Pastor, tell me is there any hope for me; can I be forgiven?" and then he threw himself to the floor and wept and wept, and almost screamed in agony. Sometimes after a confession the whole audience would break out in audible prayer, and the effect of that audience of hundreds of men praying together in audible prayer was something indescribable. Again, after another confession they would break out in uncontrollable weeping, and we would all weep, we couldn't help it. And so, the meeting went on until 2:00 a.m. with confession and weeping and praying.

At 2:00 a.m. there were still men who wished to confess, but the building had grown cold, and the Pastors involved thought it best to close the meeting. At the Tuesday noon prayer meeting, the missionaries met with hearts full of thanksgiving for the wonderful meeting of the evening before, and again asked God for greater blessings on the Tuesday evening meeting.[11]

Mr. Lee continues his account, describing the meeting on Tuesday, which opened with a message from a Korean seminary student.

After an address by Mr. Kil, our most gifted Korean preacher, we dismissed all those who wished to go home, and again nearly six hundred remained. The meeting was much the same as the Monday evening meeting, but the

---

[11] (Lee, 1907)

manifestation was greater. Some of us were praying for two men especially, Mr. Kim and Mr. Chu, for we felt that these two men had things in their lives that needed to be confessed. The climax came when Mr. Kim gained the needed strength. He was sitting on the platform, and suddenly he arose and came forward and was immediately given an opportunity. He confessed to hatred in his heart for the other brethren and especially for Mr. Blair and then he went all to pieces. It was terrible beyond description the agony that man went through. He fell to the floor and acted like a man in a fit. When he broke down the whole audience broke out in a perfect storm of weeping and they wept and wept and wept. We missionaries were weeping like the rest, and we simply couldn't keep from it.

While they were weeping Mr. Kang got up to pray, and that poor man agonized in prayer and then he broke down completely and wept as if his heart would break. The brethren gathered around put their arms about him, and soon he became quiet, then it was beautiful to see him go to Mr. Kim, put his arms lovingly about him and weep with him. When Mr. Kim broke, he turned to Mr. Blair and said: "Pastor Blair, can you forgive me, can you forgive me?" Mr. Blair got up to pray, said the word "Father" twice, and he could go no further; he was beyond words.

Mr. Blair's own words for what happened next:

It seemed as if the roof was lifted from the building and the Spirit of God came down from heaven in a mighty avalanche of power upon us. I fell at Kim's side and wept and prayed as I had never prayed before. My last glimpse of the audience is photographed indelibly on my brain. Some threw themselves full length upon the floor, hundreds stood with arms outstretched toward heaven. Every man forgot every other. Each was face to face with God. I can hear yet that fearful sound of hundreds of men pleading with God for life, for mercy. The cry went out over the city till the heathen were in consternation.[12]

And returning to Mr. Lee's account:

The audience kept on weeping, and it seemed as if they could not stop. At last we had to sing a hymn to quiet them, for we feared that some might lose control of themselves. During the singing, they quieted down and then the confessions began again, and so it went on until 2:00 a.m.

One of the most striking things of the evening was a prayer by one of the college students. He asked that he might be

---

[12] (Blair & Hunt, 1977)

allowed to make a public confession to God and was given the opportunity. In a broken voice, he began to pray, and such a prayer I never heard before. We had a vision of a human heart laid bare before its God. He confessed to adultery, hatred, lack of love for his wife and several other sins that I do not remember. As he prayed he wept; in fact, he could hardly control himself, and as he wept the audience wept with him. We all felt as if we were in the presence of the living God.[13]

These two meetings were a climax of sorts, the culmination of the many years, weeks and months of prayer, preparation, and expectation that had been slowly building since the Spirit had first been felt in a similar way in Wonsan in 1903.

Dr. Underwood's account expands on the scope of the Spirit's move:

---

[13] (Lee, 1907)

The above meetings had been held with only men present due to space constraints at the Central Church. But the Lord did not forget the women, and His power also fell upon them, as they met in a separate location. When the power was felt, the women agonized over their sins and confessed as the men had done, and on Monday and Tuesday evenings the meetings for women being continued, God's mighty power continued to be manifested. So great was the strain that one of the women became unconscious. The following morning, Mrs. Bernheisel went down to the girls' school in the city and found the Spirit there also; she wrote, "The Spirit of God literally fell on us, and we couldn't help but weep and confess our sins ."[14]

---

[14] (Underwood, 1908)

With the conference finished after the Tuesday night meeting, the missionaries wondered if the great manifestation of the Spirit encountered during the conference would end.

Rev. Lee's account continues, starting with his immediate impression upon entering the building on Wednesday evening:

> What a joy it was to find that in our four prayer meetings Wednesday evening was manifested the same mighty power... One could feel that God's Spirit was present.
>
> After a short address, all who wished to go home were dismissed. As soon as the audience was quiet we had audible prayer together, and immediately after a number of men jumped to their feet signifying an intense desire to confess their sins. After a few confessions, the climax came, when Elder Chu got the strength to make his confession. All through that wonderful Tuesday evening meeting he sat and

looked like a man who has received his death sentence. We felt sure he had some terrible sin to confess, and we prayed that God would give him strength. He had been sitting on the platform, and suddenly I found him standing beside me, and then my heart gave a bound of joy, for I knew he had surrendered and that God's Spirit was now able to cleanse him. He began in a broken voice and could hardly articulate, so moved was he. As he went on his words grew clearer, and then it all came out. He confessed to adultery and misuse of funds, and as he told of it he was in the most fearful agony I have ever seen expressed by any mortal being. He was trembling from head to foot, and I was afraid he would fall, so I put my arm about him to hold him up. In fearful distress of mind he cried out, "Was there ever such a terrible sinner as I am?" and then he beat the pulpit with his hands with all his strength. At last he sank to the floor and writhed and writhed in agony, crying for forgiveness. He looked as though he would die if he did not get relief. It was terrible to witness, but oh! it was so beautiful to see the Korean brethren gather about him, put their arms around him and comfort him in his time of anguish. As soon as Mr. Chu broke down the whole audience broke out in weeping, and they wept and wailed and wailed, and it seemed as if they couldn't stop. I had to begin a song to quiet them. We held the meeting a little longer and then dismissed the audience, thankful that God's Spirit was still manifest among us, and more than thankful that Elder Chu had obtained the strength to make his confession.[15]

Not to distract from these accounts, but to clarify, it may be helpful to note that though the reader

---

[15] (Lee, 1907)

may question the sensationalism of the above accounts, the emotional aspect of the revival was not sought by the missionaries. The primary missionaries involved were supported through Presbyterian and Methodist denominations, groups not known for using emotion to manipulate a feeling of revival. In his account of the revival, Goforth addresses this question directly:

Let man say what he will, these confessions were controlled by a power not human—either the devil or the Holy Spirit caused them, but no divinely enlightened mind can for one instant believe that the devil caused that chief man in the church to confess such a sin. It hindered the Almighty God while it remained covered, and it glorified Him as soon as it was uncovered; and so with rare exceptions did all the confessions in Korea that year.[16]

Returning to the account as documented by Dr. Underwood:

> [Fellow missionary] Mrs. Baird writes that it was a matter of regret to all that the Pyongyang college and academy was not in session at the time of the gracious visitations described above. Several of the resident students were led through a very wonderful experience, and on all sides the earnest hope was expressed and the prayer offered that the beginning of the spring term might witness another wonderful manifestation of God's power and that not one of the students might be left unvisited.
>
> Several days before the opening of the school, informal prayer meetings,

---

[16] (Goforth, 1943)

attended as well by several of the Korean members of the school faculty were held in the Principal's study. One morning, feeling burdened, he sought out a fellow missionary who had been much exercised in prayer and the two knelt together and prayed for the descent of the Spirit upon the school. It was at that hour that the storm broke in the study. Cries and sobs of anguish filled not only the room but the whole house.

For two wonderful weeks the work went on among the boys, with whom meetings were held every day at four. No attempt was made to lead these meetings. Indeed, leadership would have been impossible. All were prostrate on their faces and all alike except those who had already received a blessing were in an agony of repentance. Sometimes they beat their foreheads and heads against the floor, sometimes they literally writhed in anguish, — then when there seemed no more power of resistance left they would spring to their feet and with terrible sobs and crying pour out their confessions. No human power could have dragged these confessions to light.

So the power spread like wildfire from station to station and from little country group to group, at the country classes and among both Methodists and Presbyterians, time and space failing here to give extracts from all the thrilling reports that were sent. And now what were the results of this wonderful revival? Was it a mere wave of emotionalism? Korea had known Christianity for years but never before had anything been seen like this. What results can it show as a seal to its divine origin? "By their fruits ye shall know them," said our Lord. "Men do not gather grapes of thorns or figs of thistles." Satan does not cast out Satan, and here on all sides we see following these revivals sinners converted, those who had done wrong making confession and restitution of money and goods, the churches crowded to overflowing with inquirers and new believers, the coffers of the Lord's treasury filled, and men of different denominations lovingly joining hands, putting away old jealousies, forwarding the Lord's kingdom shoulder to shoulder.[17]

Far from being simply an interesting history lesson, this remarkable move of God provides relevant lessons to anyone with a desire to see the Spirit poured out in power. Knowledge of a historical revival may be interesting, but is ultimately of very little value if one becomes like the children of Israel who saw God's acts, rather than being as Moses who understood His ways.

Samuel Moffett, a scholar and son of one of the missionaries on the front lines of this revival,

---

[17] (Underwood, 1908)

wrote an article in 1985 challenging Presbyterians with the question, "Where's the power?"[18] Noting Jesus' words recorded in Acts that He would send power to the disciples, Moffett makes the case we should be able to expect power, even as was manifested in the Korean revival, but notes with insight the Holy Spirit cannot work through an unyielded life. Moffett admonishes Christians not to close or disconnect the faucet and still expect the water to flow forth. In other words, how can we expect the Holy Spirit to work, if we are not willing to be obedient to the requests made of us by His still, small voice?

Giving attention to this time and place where God's hand was very evident will give the astute reader a better understanding of God's ways, leading to practical considerations helpful in preparing the way for the flood of the Spirit to

---

[18] (Moffett, 1985)

come again. Before pointing out some of the lessons gleaned from considering the Korean revival, a discussion of the background and events leading up to the Korean revival may be helpful.

Background

On the eastern coast of Asia lies one of the most fascinating countries of the Far East. To the north is Manchuria, China; to the east Japan; to the south and west the vast tracts of China. In the center are the 85,000 square miles that comprise the country of Korea. The scenery of this land is beautiful; the low houses with their thatched or tiled roofs are picturesque; the people intellectual; and the manners and customs are similar in many respects to those of Palestine in the days of Christ. The history of the land goes back beyond the time of King David.

– Korean missionary in 1910 [19]

Far from being a backward people with a primitive culture (as western missionaries may have supposed), the Koreans of the late 1800s were an advanced people group. The Korean people had, independently of the Western world,

---

[19] (Davis, 1910)

developed multiple kinds of metals, art forms and religious practices, and they held to an ethical and moral code which demanded respect for age and authority. Korea is situated in a location conducive to trade, and thus, by the 1800s, had relationships with China, Russia, and Japan among others. The Korean people had endured much suffering in their varied and lengthy history, usually through oppression by China, their powerful neighbor to the North, or through warring with Japan, their rival a short boat ride away. Nevertheless, they emerged from the suffering with a strong national identity and an independent ruling monarchy.

In the late 1800s the ruling King and Queen of Korea came to realize they had fallen behind in technological advances, which were progressing at dizzying rates in the West, as America rose to power during the age of the industrial revolution. Seeking another source of relationships to

Picture 2 – Buddhism has a long history in Korea, and some still worship idols such as this one, located in a temple on the outskirts of Seoul, Korea. Photo by author, taken September 2016.

counter the ever-present threat of oppression from China, the Korean monarchy reached out to western powers such as the United States and Canada for assistance. While Koreans had previously sought to protect their rich culture through isolation and keeping others away out of fear, Korea now invited westerners to come teach their advanced skills.

The missionaries arrived in Korea at the end of the 1800s, likely unaware of the weakness felt by the prevailing government who needed the westerners' presence to offset the ever-present threat from China. The Korean government also needed the western relationships to give legitimacy to their authority, which was under recurring threat from the Japanese. The Japanese backed assassination attempts of the Korean monarch several times in the first years of the missionaries' stay in Korea. One of these assassination attempts actually opened the door wide for future ministry, as Dr. Allen, in Korea on a medical visa, saved the life of a member of the royal family and gained both trust and favor from the King and Queen. Dr. Allen's connection to the royal family allowed the missionaries to expand their efforts from caring only for the natives' physical health to their spiritual health as well.

Eventually, in 1904, the Koreans welcomed Japanese army troops to ward off an invasion from Russia. But after the Japanese gained the upper hand in the Russo-Japanese war in 1905 and beat back the Russians, rather than withdrawing their troops, the Japanese took steps to retain their hold on Korea. The Japanese formally made Korea a subject territory with their annexation in 1910, but the Japanese soldiers had been a permanent fixture since the Russo-Japanese war some five years previously.

The Japanese instituted a series of measures to solidify their influence and power over Korea. These regulations were designed to demoralize the Korean people. Regulations such as disallowing traditional Korean hair styles and forcing Japanese style dress and appearance left the people of Korea in a low place. Not only had they finally admitted how far behind they had fallen technologically, but now they were also subject again to their historical rival, and were

Picture 3 – Looking down on part of Seoul, Korea in 2016. Photo by the author, taken September 2016.

forced to abandon aspects of their rich culture they held dear.

From this state of national weakness, political instability, and public humiliation, the gospel went forth with great power and rapidity. Recognizing that these circumstances led up to the Pyongyang Revival is helpful in identifying other situations which may produce a season conducive to the Lord again stirring up his people. The Lord did not send an outpouring of His Spirit upon those full of pride and confidence, but rather gave His awesome mercies liberally to a people who were in much distress.

Keys to Revival

LORD, I have heard the report about Thee and I fear. O LORD, revive Thy work in the midst of the years, In the midst of the years make it known; In wrath remember mercy.

- Habakkuk 3:2

After seeing the Spirit move in Pyongyang first-hand, one missionary report ends, "May these floods flow every place."[20] But this remarkable and mighty move of God in Korea did not flow to every place, though it did impact the course of an entire nation. In fact, Pyongyang, Korea, the city in which this flood was poured out with such generosity, is by many accounts one of the spiritually darkest areas on earth today. The flood of the Spirit is needed again to reclaim a nation

---

[20] (Federal Council of Protestant Evangelical Missions in Korea, 1907)

full of division, whose two halves (North and South Korea) are opposites in many ways, but share a common need for a return of the Spirit in power.

The national and political situation of the Korean revival discussed above was only one part of the environment which enabled the Lord to send revival in a powerful way. There were certainly other factors as well. This book will highlight four key aspects that characterized the powerful birth and growth of the Pyongyang Revival.

Why look further at these aspects of revival, when it is only God who can send forth His Spirit? We are told "the eyes of the LORD move to and fro throughout the earth that He may strongly support those whose heart is completely His," so it becomes clear the Lord is willing, even desiring, to send forth His Spirit when His people are willing to prepare the way (2 Chron 16:9). He is a God who knows how to give good gifts to His children (Matt 7:11), and He will give the Holy Spirit to those who ask Him (Luke 11:13).

Since God is willing to give the Holy Spirit to those who ask, we often do not have the blessing because we either do not ask, or we ask with wrong motives (James 4:2-3). Considering how the Lord was entreated to send revival on Pyongyang over a century ago may clarify for us the proper way to seek revival here and now.

Charles Finney, known as the father of American revivalism, was particularly adamant that the Lord would send revival if His people would only do their part:

> I said that a revival is the result of the right use of the appropriate means. The means which God has enjoined for the production of a revival, doubtless have a natural tendency to produce a revival. Otherwise God would not have enjoined them. But means will not produce a

revival, we all know, without the blessing of God. No more will grain, when it is sowed, produce a crop without the blessing of God. It is impossible for us to say that there is not as direct an influence or agency from God, to produce a crop of grain, as there is to produce a revival. What are the laws of nature according to which it is supposed that grain yields a crop? They are nothing but the constituted manner of the operations of God. In the Bible, the word of God is compared to grain, and preaching is compared to sowing seed, and the results to the springing up and growth of the crop. And the result is just as philosophical in the one case, as in the other, and is as naturally connected with the cause; or, more correctly, a revival is as naturally a result of the use of the appropriate means as a crop is of the use of its appropriate means.

I wish this idea to be impressed on all your minds, for there has long been an idea prevalent that promoting religion has something very peculiar in it, not to be judged of by the ordinary rules of cause and effect; in short, that there is no connection of the means with the result, and no tendency in the means to produce the effect. No doctrine is more dangerous than this to the prosperity of the church, and nothing more absurd.

Suppose a man were to go and preach this doctrine among farmers, about their sowing grain. Let him tell them that God is a sovereign, and will give them a crop only when it pleases him, and that for them to plow and plant and labor as if they expected to raise a crop is very wrong, and taking the work out of the hands of God, that it interferes with his sovereignty, and is going on in their own strength: and that there is no connection between the means and the result on which they can depend. And now, suppose the farmers should believe such doctrine. Why, they would starve the world to death.

Just such results will follow from the church's being persuaded that promoting religion is somehow so mysteriously a subject of Divine sovereignty, that there is no natural connection between the means and the end. What are the results? Why, generation after generation has gone down to hell. No doubt more than five thousand millions have gone down to hell, while the church has been dreaming, and waiting for God to save them without the use of means. It has been the devil's most successful means of destroying souls. The connection is as clear in religion as it is when the farmer sows his grain. . . . and I fully believe that could facts be known, it would be found that when the appointed means have been rightly used, spiritual blessings have been obtained with greater uniformity than temporal ones.[21]

Thus, not only is it possible for the Lord to send forth His Spirit again in a mighty way, as He did in Pyongyang, but the Lord also wants to honor His people who prepare the way for His Spirit to come. The Lord desires to bless those who humble themselves and ask Him for more of His Spirit. In the words of Christ, "how much more shall your Father who is in heaven give what is good to those who ask Him!" (Matt 7:11).

Having this confidence, let us look at and learn from four key aspects of the preparation which preceded the great Pyongyang Revival. As we entreat the Lord for revival today, may we look to the Word of God in full sincerity, offer up faith-filled prayers in desperation, gain a spiritual perspective of God's interests, and humble

---

[21] (Finney, 1835)

ourselves to confess whatever things of the heart on which the Spirit places His finger.

1ˢᵗ Key – the Word of God

For as the rain and the snow come down from heaven, and do not return there without watering the earth, and making it bear and sprout, and furnishing seed to the sower and bread to the eater; so shall My word be which goes forth from My mouth; It shall not return to Me empty, without accomplishing what I desire, and without succeeding in the matter for which I sent it.

- Isaiah 55:10-11

Though in the 1880s Korea was a nation closed to outside influence, and the massacre of Korean Catholic converts in the 1860s was still a fresh memory, there were Christians who were looking for opportunity to bring the good news of the gospel to this " hermit kingdom. " Author and

Picture 4 - Jeoldusan Martyrs' Shrine, a Catholic memorial erected on the site of the mass murder of Korean Catholics in 1866. Photo by the author, taken September 2016.

missionary George Davis explains that one such man, Henry Loomis, agent of the American Bible Society in Yokohama, met a Korean in Japan, and in 1885 had this Korean expatriate translate the gospel of Mark into his native tongue.[22]

Davis does a particularly good job of explaining the prominent role Scripture played in the evangelization of Korea:

> When American missionaries, Dr. H. G. Underwood, Dr. H. G. Appenzeller, and Dr. W. B. Scranton, passed through Japan they were given a few copies of the gospel of Mark in Korean, which they had in their hands when they first reached the shores of Korea.[23]

This was actually not the first Scripture to reach Korea in the native tongue. Davis continues:

---

[22] (Davis, 1910)

[23] (Davis, 1910)

In 1875, Dr. John Ross and Rev. John Mclntyre, Scottish Presbyterian missionaries working in Manchuria, a region of China just north of the Korean border, came into contact with Koreans who had gone across the border for business purposes. These missionaries learned Koreans could read and understand the Chinese translation of the Scriptures. A scholarly Korean was engaged to make a translation from the Chinese into the vernacular language of Korea, under the direction of Dr. Ross and Mr. Mclntyre.

In 1882 an edition of the Gospels of Luke and John were published, but it was difficult to circulate them in Korea. Books of a foreign religion were not allowed to come into the Hermit Kingdom, and [after] the books were printed, the problem was how to get them into the country.

Korean merchants came into China periodically to buy the old official papers which were offered for sale, and brought them back into Korea on the backs of coolies. The suggestion came to Dr. Ross and Mr. Mclntyre that if the Scriptures were made up into bundles, unbound, they might be carried into the country without detection. It was in this manner that God's Word in Korean was first introduced into the country. . . .

Saw Sang Yun, had the honor of being the first Korean colporteur.[24] In 1883 he left [China] with a load of Scriptures, with instructions to reach Seoul with them if possible. After varied experiences he was successful in reaching the capital with only a few copies in his hand. He

---

[24] Someone employed by a religious society to distribute Bibles.

remained here until after the arrival of the American missionaries in 1885. [25]

[Thus,] it was the Ross translation which laid the foundation of the translation work in Korea. Between 1883 and 1886 no less than 15,690 copies of this translation were circulated in Korea through the colporteurs. From the beginning the work of Saw, the colporteur, was very successful. Dr. Ross writes that the first congregation of Korean converts were almost entirely those led to Christ by Saw.[26]

Once missionaries were able to settle inside Korea, a board of translators was formed, which by 1900 produced a tentative version of the New Testament. In 1906 an authorized version of the

---

[25] (Davis, 1910)

[26] (Davis, 1910)

New Testament was completed and published.[27] This translation work and the groundwork of the earlier circulated copies were both integral to the timing and scope of the revival in Korea.

The missionaries in Korea began with the Word of God already in hand in the native language, so perhaps it should be no surprise that they enjoyed seeing a faster harvest of souls than those laboring in other parts of Asia. Sending the Word of God into Korea on the backs of native Koreans had the effect of an artillery bombardment, softening the way for the arrival of ground troops.

The reliance upon the Scripture and the devotion to quickly translate the remainder of the Bible continued to bear much spiritual fruit. Can we doubt the central importance of God's word when we consider that the Pyongyang Revival began

---

[27] (Davis, 1910)

only months after the 1906 publication of the authorized New Testament?

One Korean missionary interviewed by Davis stated:

> From the commencement of Mission work in Korea the printed page of God's Word has occupied a peculiarly prominent place. The Korean Christian is a man of one book, and that book, the Bible. The secret of the strength of the Korean Church lies in the fact that it has been nourished on the Word of God.[28]

> For years, the almost universal custom of the Korean Christians was to carry a New Testament with them, and they eagerly linked themselves with the world-wide movement of the Pocket Testament League. This movement was a plan for linking together people throughout the

---

[28] (Davis, 1910)

world to read a portion of God's Word daily; to carry it about with one; and to give it to the unsaved to win them to Christ.[29]

In these years of exponential growth of the Church in Korea, the Word of God was often the only teacher to bring people to Christ. For example, it was reported a man from a rural district had heard the Gospel in the city and took a Testament home with him. He kept on reading it to his neighbors until more than fifty believed. Then they felt they ought to form a church, but did not know how. From the New Testament they inferred that the door of entrance was by the use of water in baptism, but they were at a loss as to how it was applied. So after consultation they decided that each would go home and take a bath and then meet

---

[29] (Davis, 1910)

and form their church. The missionary documenting the report had no doubt that God was pleased.[30]

A cornerstone of the missionaries' work in Korea was a system of Bible training classes. The plan for these classes was originated almost at the commencement of mission work in Korea, and the land was full of these unique gatherings. They were not Bible classes held each Sunday throughout the year, but were annual Bible conferences lasting for a week or ten days. The Koreans frequently walked a hundred miles or more to attend the gatherings. They paid all their own expenses, and then for ten days delighted in the study of God's Word.[31]

---

[30] (Goforth, 1943)

[31] (Davis, 1910)

Perhaps the impact of these Bible conferences is obvious already, but Davis points out:

> It was in the midst of a Bible conference [in Pyongyang] . . . that the Spirit of God had fallen upon the community in such a manner . . . which stirred the whole Christian world.

> The Koreans not only read the Bible, and used the Bible to bring others to Christ, but they also memorized the Word of God with a passion. After the revival, it was reported that two little girls in Pyongyang learned and recited the entire New Testament with the exception of the Gospel of Matthew, while a number of others learned from 400 to 4000 verses.[32]

Jonathan Goforth expands on the importance of Scripture in the revival:

---

[32] (Davis, 1910)

At the time of the revival, Bibles could not be printed fast enough. In one year at Pyongyang, 6,000 Bibles were sold. Everyone learned it . . . and Christians traveling on business always carried the Bible along. Along the way, and at the inns, they opened it up and read, and many were attracted and saved.

The Koreans had a proverb that the elders have the right to criticize the juniors, then when they get through, if there is anything left of the juniors, they may in turn criticize the elders. After being saved, the Koreans decided the oldest criticism of man is in the Bible; therefore they let the Bible criticize them first, and they never find anything of themselves left so as to venture afterwards to criticize God's Book.[33]

---

[33] (Goforth, 1943)

> If men were all humble enough to approach the Bible in the Korean spirit, there would be more books burned around some seminaries than ever were burned on the streets of Ephesus when Paul was there. It would cause world-wide revival.[34]

From understanding the spread of the written Word of God in Korea, we can see the Word of God occupied an appropriately prominent place in the Korean Church. The Word was a key to preparing the way for the Pyongyang Revival, and also the key to its spread and continuation. New believers rightly valued the Word of God, and spent much time in reading, discussing, and memorizing this precious printed material. In a day and age when the Word is often at our fingertips, do we treat the Word with the respect and preciousness it deserves?

---

[34] (Goforth, 1943)

Picture 5 – Bibles for sale in Seoul, Korea about 110 years after the New Testament was translated. Photo by the author, taken September 2016.

2nd Key – Prayer

So then, those who had received his word
were baptized; and that day there were
added about three thousand souls. They
were continually devoting themselves to
the apostles' teaching and to fellowship,
to the breaking of bread and to prayer.

- Acts 2:41-4

Any student of revival will be unsurprised by the integral nature of prayer in preparing the way for the Pyongyang Revival. Prayer ushered in, and then sustained, the revival as expressed in the accounts below. To get a complete picture of the role played by prayer, it is necessary to back up to the year 1904, three years before the climax of the revival occurred.

Dr. Underwood describes in her writings how a joint Methodist and Presbyterian conference was held in August of 1904 and again in 1905, each time with the Spirit filling all attendees with "holy love to the Lord and to each other," which gave much desire for a unified work of Christ in Korea regardless of denominational grounds.[35]

Soon after the conference of 1905, several of the missionaries and native Korean Christians from the city of Wonsan received "a baptism of the Holy Spirit with power, characterized by a deep and searching sense of sin and God's awful holiness and majesty" according to Dr. Underwood's account.[36] This fresh zeal, combined with news of the Welsh Revival of 1904 and moves of the Spirit in India and other places, created an increased spiritual appetite for the

---

[35] (Underwood, 1908)

[36] (Underwood, 1908)

Picture 6 – Gravestone of Dr. Lillias Underwood, whose writings are quoted extensively throughout this book. She and her husband were the first of four generations of the Underwood family to serve in Korea. Located in Yanghwajin Foreign Missionary Cemetery, Seoul, Korea. Photo by the author, taken September 2016.

Spirit to come work with power in Korea as well.[37]

This newfound spiritual zeal and appetite naturally expressed itself in prayer, as Dr. Underwood documents so well:

> Sometime in the Fall of 1905, a little printed pledge to pray daily for the outpouring of the Spirit on the Korean missionaries, on the native Christians and on the heathen communities, was sent by one of the Southern Presbyterians to each missionary in Korea to be signed and kept if he wished. It was simply putting into definite form the leading of the Spirit in all our hearts, a united cry, "Bless me, even me also, O my father!" (Gen 27:34) It was the cry heard in our little circles of prayer. It was the continued petition of our closets, the principal thought and

---

[37] (Underwood, 1908)

desire filling our conscious moments. The natives were moved as one man with us. Some of the little churches held nightly meetings of prayer for this blessing. For months, even years, some had been holding these meetings before the foreigners began.[38]

The heart petitions for greater blessing solidified into regular requests for the Lord to send revival to the Korean peninsula:

> The women in some of the churches met regularly to pray for revival. This was the chief theme of their requests at all their services. How they prayed in secret none but God knows, but each man and woman knew how he or she was led to besiege the throne, with a spirit that would not be denied, that with fasting and strong

---

[38] (Underwood, 1908)

crying, they continued in supplication before God.

This prayer was divinely led, for even as the blessing was demanded, as it were, the weak flesh wondered how such large things as we were irresistibly impelled to ask could possibly be expected. There were prayers for Pentecostal outpourings; that thousands should turn to Christ; that the great class of the nobility, (at that time still yet untouched), so bound down by caste, by custom and social usage, by political requirements and family duties and bonds, should come into the kingdom; that the church should be spiritualized; that Koreans, intellectually converted, should realize the hideousness of sin; and that we, natives and foreigners, might "comprehend with all saints what is the breadth and length and height and depth, and to know the love of Christ that surpasses knowledge, that you may be filled up to all the fulness of God" (Eph

3:18-19). These were the prayers that had been unitedly offered by all the missionaries at the conferences held every year since August, 1904, at the churches, native and foreign, at family worship, in little neighborhood prayer meetings, in the closet and as they walked the streets or went about their work.[39]

Dr. Underwood was not alone in recognizing the time spent beseeching the Lord for the blessing of the Spirit and for revival. Jonathan Goforth notes in his book, "The missionaries spent one to several hours each day for months in preparing a way in their hearts for the Holy Spirit."[40] Continuing with her account, Dr. Underwood writes of several missionaries whose messages at conferences assisted in developing the common

---

[39] (Underwood, 1908)

[40] (Goforth, 1943)

burden on the hearts of those ministering in Korea:

In August, 1906, a Bible and prayer conference was held at Pyongyang, by the missionaries of that station, for the deepening of their own spiritual life. Dr. Hardie, of Wonsan, was present and helped them greatly, and [missionary] Mr. Lee writes that there was born in their hearts the desire that God would take complete control of their lives and use them mightily in His service. Immediately after this, at Seoul, during the Annual Meeting of the Presbyterian missionaries, many of them received much blessing and aid in meeting Dr. Howard Agnew Johnston, a visiting mission board representative, who had already been greatly used in helping the Seoul missionaries. He went to Pyongyang later and stirred up fervent desire in the hearts of native Christians by telling them of the wonderful blessing poured into India, "and from that time natives and missionaries were praying for the blessing, till it came," says Mr. Lee. To one looking back over the whole history of events, it had already begun. [41]

The blessing thus began to be poured out upon the people as the people poured out their hearts to God in prayer. Jonathan Goforth adds illustrations of the dedication of the people to prayer and the outcome of these desperate pleas for the Spirit:

A Bible distributor from Kang Kai, away up among the pine forests along the Yalu, also heard Dr. Johnston. He went home and told the Kang Kai church of 250 believers that the Holy Spirit alone could make effective the finished work of the Lord Jesus Christ, and that He was promised them as freely as any other gift

---

[41] (Underwood, 1908)

of God. They honored God and appreciated the gift of the Holy Spirit by meeting in the church for prayer at five o'clock, not five o'clock every evening, but every morning, through the fall and winter of 1906-7. They honored God the Holy Spirit by six months of prayer; and then He came as a flood.

As missionary and pastor Mr. Swallen said, "It paid well to have spent the several months in prayer, for when God the Holy Spirit came He accomplished more in half a day than all of us missionaries could have accomplished in half a year. In less than two months more than two thousand heathen were converted." It is always so as soon as God gets first place; but, as a rule, the Church, which professes to be Christ's, will not cease her busy round of activities and give

God a chance by waiting upon Him in prayer.[42]

During the actual revival, the prayers became so urgent the people could no longer wait for another to finish praying, but all lifted their voices aloud in unison:

> During the revival meetings, a first-hand report noted that the room was full of men each lifting their voice to God in prayer, and most of the men in the room were praying aloud. Some were crying and pleading God's forgiveness for certain sins which they named to Him in prayer. All were pleading for the infilling of the Holy Ghost. Although there were so many voices there was no confusion at all. It was all a subdued perfect harmony, not easily explained with words.[43]

---

[42] (Goforth, 1943)

[43] (Underwood, 1908)

Then, in addition to its role in preparing the way for revival, Goforth expands on the integral nature of prayer to the continuation of the revival as well:

> Just as did the Church in Acts, the early Korean Church put great reliance in prayer. One week during the revival a group of students were resisting the Holy Spirit at the high school. Another group of students had such a burden of prayer upon them for their peers that they were almost transformed in appearance, and continued in fasting and prayer until victory came. At that time in the lower schools the spirit of prayer was so powerful that the schools had to be closed for a time. The tears were falling from the children's eyes as they pored over their books.[44]

---

[44] (Goforth, 1943)

Dr. Underwood also directly comments on the reality of prayer within the revival:

> The battle was between our God and His forces on one hand and all the hosts of Satan on the other. Students who had received a blessing spent hours of every day in prayer and some spent whole nights on their faces before God.[45]

Goforth continues his commentary on the method of prayer used during the time of the revival:

> The missionaries readily admitted the Korean Christians outdistanced them in prayer. Korean Christians would commonly spend half the night in prayer. Their general practice was to get up for prayer long before dawn. A missionary was once out at in a rural area and arranged that all should meet for prayer

---

[45] (Underwood, 1908)

the next morning at five o'clock. At five o'clock the next morning he came and found three kneeling in prayer. The missionary knelt down, supposing the others had not yet arrived. After praying for some time, one of those present told him he had arrived too late. The prayer meeting had finished before he came, despite the fact some had to journey across a mountain range to be present.[46]

"Do you suppose if Christians really believed the words of the Lord Jesus, 'Where two or three meet in my name, there am I,' they could keep away?" Goforth asks rhetorically. "The Master cannot but take note of our prayer condition... Do we really believe in God the Holy Spirit? Let us be honest. Not to the extent of getting up at five o'clock through six months of cold weather to

---

[46] (Goforth, 1943)

seek Him!"[47]

Yet it was just this kind of prayer which preceded the great revival in Pyongyang. Was this prayer costly? Undoubtedly so, with many Koreans leaving their warm beds in the middle of the night, and many missionaries sacrificing hours of their day to spend on their knees, all together petitioning their Lord for a great outpouring of His Spirit. They knew God was not limited to the success of their past results, and they were filled with a godly dissatisfaction with the status-quo. A compassion for the unsaved and a desperation for more of the Spirit drove them to their Lord at all hours of the day and night for weeks, months, and in some cases, even years before they were enveloped by the flood of the Spirit.

So was devoting themselves to nothing but prayer worth the cost: all the nights of lost sleep, sore

---

[47] (Goforth, 1943)

knees, missed family time, and sacrificed opportunities? In this case, the end results are known—the cost can be weighed against the eternal value of the thousands of human souls ushered into the Kingdom of God. But is the cost worth it to us today, in our time and place, when we do not yet know the end result?

3rd Key – Heavenly Perspective

> *If Christians have deep feeling on the subject of religion themselves, they will produce deep feeling wherever they go. And if they are cold, or light and trifling, they inevitably destroy all deep feeling, even in awakened sinners.*

> - Charles Finney, 1835 [48]

Those preparing for the outpouring of the Holy Spirit in Korea were filled with a desperation for more of the Lord. Their consuming desire to see the Lord's power satisfy the great need in Korea gave them a heavenly perspective which influenced the practical aspects of their lives. Rather than being focused on earthly matters, the believers in Korea had heaven's priorities constantly in mind. The eternal value of human souls was so clear to these believers that temporal

---

[48] (Finney, 1835)

matters were held lightly. Sacrifices in the physical realm were made with gladness because of the spiritual focus held by the missionaries and Korean converts. No longer were the missionaries Presbyterians and Methodists, but they were brothers and sisters in Christ, serving Him together. No longer were the Korean converts concerned with the business of this life, but rather they were fully concerned with making sure their friends, neighbors and even the strangers passing by in the street had a chance to meet the God of the universe who had died for them. No longer did the Christians count their wealth and possessions as their own, but rather they gave liberally to meet the needs of the Lord's house first.

Many aspects of how this heavenly perspective changed the lives of those influenced by the revival are already clear from the accounts described above. There are many more firsthand accounts that describe how the unity of the saints and the consecration of the believers led Christians into much evangelism and expressions of generosity with time and money. Some of these accounts are included in the following passages, to add additional insight into the powerful impact this revival had on the Korean peninsula.

Dr. Underwood records many details about how believers gained a greater understanding of unity within the body of Christ during the revival, and how opposition to this unity was overcome. Describing the lead-up to the revival, she notes:

> The beginning of revival in Korea was at the conference for prayer and consecration held by all the American missionaries of both Methodist and Presbyterian denominations in Seoul, August, 1904. There had come upon all present, unexpectedly, overwhelmingly, a powerful impulse toward closer fellowship and entire union in work, and the conviction that the native Church in

Korea ought emphatically to be one. Men were swept away with an irresistible tide of enthusiasm. No one wished or attempted to resist the mighty movement of the Spirit. All who were present testified to the blessed sense of the presence of the Spirit of Love.

It was a blessed experience, but, as might have been expected, the powers of evil would never quietly submit without interference to a measure so calculated for their overthrow, so in keeping with the Lord's will, and there forthwith sprang up in the minds of a few, difficulties, doubts, mistrusts and hindrances. Nevertheless, a similar meeting was held in August, 1905. A Union Council was then regularly organized with officers and rules. Plans were made and various committees formed to forward and perfect the organization of one United Native Church of Christ in the near future. Again one Spirit seemed to fill all hearts. One impulse of holy love to our Lord and to each other seemed to move us all to one supreme consummation — obedience to the dying command of the Master, and we all felt that He would follow this with still greater blessings.[49]

Dr. Underwood continues commenting on the theme of unity when she documents the prayer meetings occurring in the immediate lead-up to the revival:

We missionaries had our union meetings with the Methodists one week before the class began. They were a source of the richest blessing to all of us and when we were closing Thursday evening it being suggested that we continue the meetings for the next week or so at noontime, we decided to do so. Daily we have been waiting there and praying for the Holy

---

[49] (Underwood, 1908)

Spirit. We have no leader for the meeting. Each one who enters the room quietly kneels down and as he is led prays. We find that these meetings of ours are blessed just in proportion as we spend the whole time from first to last on our knees in prayer or proffering requests for prayer or thanksgiving, precluding much conversation or discussion, even upon the progress or incidents of the revival.[50]

As might be expected, there were also challenges to this wonderful unity, and Dr. Underwood described how this opposition was removed by prayer and the conviction of the Holy Spirit:

A Methodist preacher had longed for a blessing on his people and when it fell first on the Presbyterians, he was jealous and displeased, and it was feared in several quarters that he was using his

---

[50] (Underwood, 1908)

influence both in the pulpit and the classroom to throw discredit on the movement. Special prayer was therefore made for him by native and foreign members of both denominations.

On Friday evening the break in the Methodist ranks began. One young man after another, members of a band who had agreed together that they would stand out against the prevailing influences, gave up all pretence of resistance and cast themselves on the Lord for mercy. At midnight there were as many as fifty risen to their feet awaiting their turn to confess their sins. During the evening many threw themselves on their knees before the preacher and confessed that they had done wrong in yielding to his influence. Conviction seized upon him and at the close of the meeting this proud man was weeping in the arms of the missionaries and sobbing out penitent confessions of coldness, willfulness and jealousies.

During the remaining evenings there was little disposition to resist the Holy Spirit. Then the Lord began pouring out His blessings upon the Methodist congregations in the city and the same wonderful manifestations were exhibited here that had been seen elsewhere.[51]

Looking back at this revival, it is easy to miss the significance of the unity within the body of Christ in Korea, and the role it played in preparing the way for the revival. Missionaries are expected to have a single-minded focus on the Gospel when traveling to a foreign land, so one might expect working with Christians from a different denomination would have been normal.

It must be remembered, however, that many of these missionaries were allowed into Korea not as full time preachers, but as medical professionals

---

[51] (Underwood, 1908)

or as professors or teachers. The missionaries had to find time to learn the Korean language, perform the functions required of them as doctors, nurses, professors and teachers, as well as learn how to survive in a land with foreign customs and foreign foods. There were no simple household tasks, but everything was complicated by a second language and unfamiliar customs. Then, in this environment, where just surviving daily life was a struggle, the missionaries were expected to make converts. They needed to send back news of their progress to their mission board and supporters back home. They needed to show what wonderful work was being done to justify the expense of sending them halfway around the world.

In situations such as these, it would only be natural for the missionaries to become territorial, defending their progress against workers from another mission board, yet instead they gained a

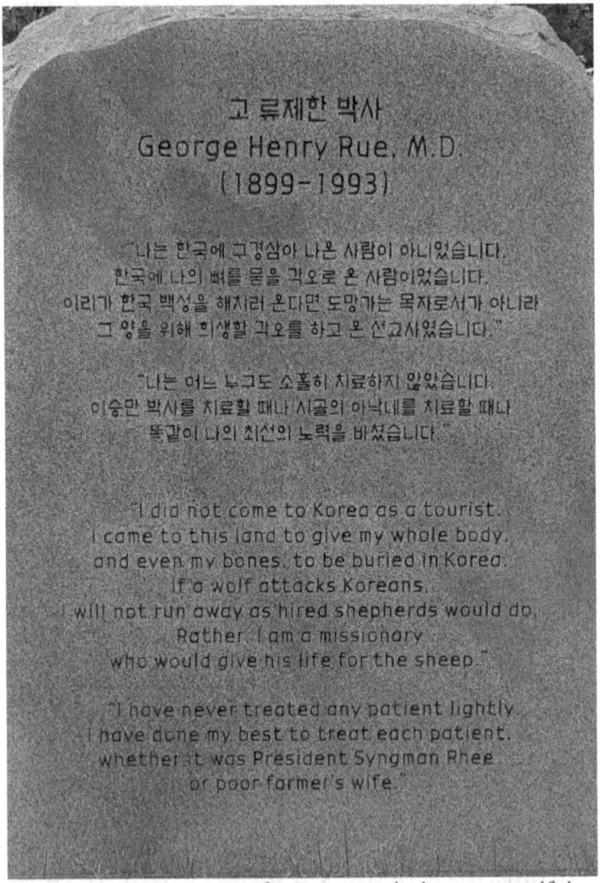

Picture 7 – Gravestone of a Korean missionary, testifying to the spiritual perspective typical of those who served in Korea. "I did not come to Korea as a tourist. I came to this land to give my whole body . . . I am a missionary who would give his life for the sheep." Located in Yanghwajin Foreign Missionary Cemetery, Seoul, Korea. Photo by the author, taken September 2016.

heavenly perspective that enabled them to recognize and participate in the unity of the Body of Christ, working together for Christ to be glorified through His Church in Korea.

Working together from a place of unity, the foreign missionaries and the local converts had a clear quest to bring the light of the gospel to this pagan land, and they did this with great passion, as Jonathan Goforth so clearly describes:

> A burning zeal to make known the merits of the Saviour was a special mark of the Church at Pentecost. The same is not less true of the Korean Church. It was said that the heathen complained that they could not endure the persecution of the Christians. They were evermore telling of the strong points of their Saviour. Some declared they would have to sell out and

move to some district where there were no Christians, in order to get rest.[52]

A missionary in Manchuria, China sent two evangelists over to Pyongyang to find out all about the revival. When they returned, he asked if the missionaries had opened many street chapels. The evangelists replied, "None at all. They do not need them because every Christian is a street chapel." Christian workmen have been known to spend a summer in a country where there were no Christians in order to evangelize it. Merchants as they travel from place to place are always telling the wondrous story. A hat merchant, converted in a revival on the east coast when we were there, had within a year afterwards started up little Christian communities in about a dozen places. In one of them there were

---

[52] (Goforth, 1943)

seventeen converts. A student got a month's holiday and spent the time in an un-evangelized district and won a hundred souls for God. Another student resolved to speak each day to at least six persons of their soul's salvation. By the end of nine months he had spoken to three thousand! It would take some of us homeland Christians a lifetime to speak to so many. . . .

Even little tots of schoolboys, eight and nine years of age, as soon as school was dismissed, would go out on the streets and, taking hold of the passers-by by the sleeves, would plead with tears that they yield to Jesus the Saviour. Said he, "During the last three or four days, fully four hundred men have come and confessed Christ." It was the intense pleading of the boys that cut them to the heart.

There was a man who, while visiting the city, was converted and confessed the Lord Jesus Christ in baptism. Then he went to tell his wonderful story. His clan received it in anger, and soon the enraged relatives fell upon him and beat him almost to death. When he was brought to the hospital his life hung by a thread. At the end of many weeks the doctor told him he could go home, but told him that his life might end with a hemorrhage any day. That Christian bought a great quantity of books and went home. For three years he went about his home district, giving away his books and telling of his Saviour. Then there came a day when his blood flowed out and his soul ascended to his God. But in that heathen country, where they had tried to murder him, he left eleven churches.[53]

---

[53] (Goforth, 1943)

This dedication to personal evangelism could only come from knowing the spiritual value of each soul. Korean Christians realized they could not let time or money stand in the way of evangelism once they weighed these costs against the eternal worth of each person who came to know Christ. In addition to his comments on the evangelism of the early Korean church, Goforth remarks admiringly on the financial generosity of these believers:

> Abounding liberality was another very striking characteristic of the Early Church. The Korean Christians abound in that, too. At one place a missionary told me that he dared not mention money to his people for they were giving too much now. I should like to meet the pastor in favored Christendom who could truly say that of his people. The year I was at that center the people were supporting 139 workers, male and female, teachers and preachers, and that year alone they

increased the workers by 57. That missionary said, "When we found our church was too small, we met to plan for the erection of one that would hold 1,500. The people present gave all the money they had. The men gave their watches and the women stripped off their jewelry. Others gave title deeds to portions of land. They gave all they had and wept because they couldn't give more, and they built their church free of debt."

A missionary was once at a very poor center when the leaders told him how inconvenient it was to be worshiping in private houses, but now they had a fine site offered them for $30. "Capital!" said the missionary, "go ahead and buy it." "But, Pastor," said they, "we are extremely poor here. You didn't understand us. We should like it if you would put up the money." "No," said the missionary, "you must buy your church's foundation. It will do you lots of good." However the men pleaded poverty.[54]

Then the sisters said, "If the men have no plan we think we can buy it." They took off all their jewelry and sold it, but it brought only $10. Nothing daunted, however, this woman sold a brass kettle, that one sold two brass bowls, and another sold a few pairs of brass chopsticks, for all their cooking and eating utensils are made of brass. The whole, when sold, brought $20. Now, with $30 in their hands, the women secured the church site. Since it is more blessed to give than to receive, the women received an enlarged vision. The needs of their sisters, without God and without hope, in the countless villages all around, fired their hearts and so they decided to raise $6 a month and send out a woman evangelist.

---

[54] (Goforth, 1943)

At another place the missionary was present at the dedication of a new church. It was found that there was still $50 owing on the church. A member present arose and said, "Pastor, I will next Sunday bring $50 to pay off that debt." The missionary, knowing the man was very poor, said, "Don't think of doing it yourself. We will all join together and can soon pay it off." There are churches in the homeland that are not ashamed nor afraid to carry a $50,000 debt. Next Sunday arrived and this poor Christian brought the $50. The missionary, astonished, asked, "Where did you get the money?" The Christian replied, "Pastor, don't mind. It is all clean money." Some weeks later the missionary, touring in that region, came to this man's home. On asking the man's wife where her husband was, she said, "Out in the field plowing." The missionary, on going out to the field, found the old father holding the plow handles while his son was pulling the plow. The missionary, in amazement, said, "Why, what have you done with your mule?" Said the Christian, "I couldn't bear to have the Church of Jesus Christ owing a $50 debt to a heathen, so I sold my mule to wipe it out."[55]

With such sacrifices, the clarity of these believers on the reality of their faith is quite clear. No human reasoning or dead religious tradition could have caused the great impact occurring in conjunction with the move of the Spirit in Pyongyang. The heavenly perspective held by these dear saints gave them clear priorities for how to order their lives. Some of this work began in the lives of the missionaries leading up to the revival, with a practical understanding of the unity of all believers laying the foundation for the move of the Spirit in Pyongyang. Once the

---

[55] (Goforth, 1943)

foundation was laid, further aspects of this heavenly perspective manifested themselves during the revival itself: the emphasis on evangelism and the corresponding gifts of time and money. The sacrifices made by Korean believers gave the revival power to grow and spread.

4th Key – Conviction and Confession

A revival always includes conviction of sin on the part of the church. Backslidden professors cannot wake up and begin right away in the service of God, without deep searchings of heart. The fountains of sin need to be broken up. In a true revival, Christians are always brought under such convictions; they see their sins in such a light, that often they find it impossible to maintain a hope of their acceptance with God. It does not always go to that extent; but there are always, in a genuine revival, deep convictions of sin, and often cases of abandoning all hope.

- Charles Finney, 1835 [56]

Conviction, confession and repentance also played a key role in bringing the Korean revival to fruition. The Holy Spirit never forces His way into our hearts, but rather waits to be invited into our lives. The Spirit descended as a dove upon our

---

[56] (Finney, 1835)

Lord Jesus at His baptism (Matt 3:16), and like a dove, would never be so bold as to arrive uninvited. Rather, he waits for our voluntary obedience to confess our sins in repentance before doing His work of forgiveness and cleansing from all unrighteousness (1 John 1:9). So it was in Pyongyang, where the critical moment, just before the Spirit fell in power, was the confession of sin by a church leader:

A few of us knew that there had been hatred in the hearts of some of the prominent men of the church, especially between a Mr. Kang and Mr. Kim, and we hoped that it would all come out and be confessed during these meetings. Monday night Mr. Kang got the strength and told how he had hated Mr. Kim and asked to be forgiven. It was wonderful to see that proud, strong man break down and then control himself and then break down again as he tried to tell how he had hated Mr. Kim.[57]

Dr. Underwood details the level of conviction within the revival meetings, with men (and women in other meetings) succumbing to the overwhelming realization of the wickedness of their sin:

> The wonderful manifestation of God's presence was marked, as had been those isolated incidents in Wonsan and Mokpo, by "a spirit of prayer," conviction of sin, confession and intercession. Awful and overwhelming conviction of sin was its most marked feature. Men wept, groaned, beat their breasts, falling to the ground

---

[57] (Lee, 1907)

Figure 1 - "The truth shall set you free" This is the motto for Yonsei University, established by missionaries as part of their secular reason for being in Korea before evangelism was officially allowed. Photo by the author, taken September 2016.

and writing in agony.[58]

Mr. Blair, at the center of the breakthrough that night of revival in Pyongyang, remembered the terrible necessity of the confession:

> Then [after Mr. Kim had publicly asked him for forgiveness] began a meeting the like of which I had never seen before, nor wish to see again unless in God's sight it is absolutely necessary. Every sin a human being can commit was publicly confessed that night. Pale and trembling with emotion, in agony of mind and body, guilty souls, standing in the white light of that judgment, saw themselves as God saw them. Their sins rose up in all their vileness, till shame and grief and self-loathing took complete possession; pride was driven out, the face of men forgotten. Looking up to heaven, to Jesus whom

---

[58] (Underwood, 1908)

they had betrayed, they smote themselves and cried out with bitter wailing: "Lord, Lord, cast us not away forever!" Everything else was forgotten, nothing else mattered. The scorn of men, the penalty of law, even death itself seemed of small consequence if only God forgave. . . . I know now that when the Spirit of God falls upon guilty souls, there will be confession, and no power on earth can stop it.[59]

Conviction continued to mark the revival as it spread in the coming weeks, but this conviction could be resisted. The Spirit delayed coming into some people's lives until they had yielded in obedience and confessed their sin:

The missionaries at Pyongyang honored God the Holy Spirit in their high school. They had a school of 318 students, and

---

[59] (Blair & Hunt, 1977)

that Monday morning of the opening, in February, 1907, the two missionaries in charge were early at prayer in the principal's room. They wanted the Holy Spirit to control the school from the start. They knew that if He did not control, the school would only turn out educated rascals who would be a menace to Korea. . . . Before nine o'clock had struck, that Monday morning, in the Pyongyang high school, the Spirit of the Lord was smiting those boys with conviction. Agonized cries were heard upstairs and down. Soon the principal's room was filled with boys agonized over sin. School could not be opened that day, nor the next, and Friday still found it unopened. By Friday evening the Presbyterian boys had all come through to victory, but it was clear that something held the Methodist boys back.

It all came out that evening, when about a dozen of the Methodist boys went and pleaded with their native pastor to free them from their promise to him. It seems that this Korean pastor was jealous because the revival had not started in the Methodist church. He got the high school boys to oppose it, and to resist all public confession as from the devil. But by Friday night their agony of mind was unbearable, hence their pleading to be set free from their promise.[60]

With that, the pastor went and flung himself at the missionaries' feet and confessed that the devil had filled him with envy because the revival had commenced among the Presbyterians. A missionary told me that it was dreadful to hear the confessions wrung from those students that week; that it was as if the lid of hell had been pulled off, and every imaginable sin laid bare. By the following

---

[60] (Goforth, 1943)

Monday the students were right with God, with their teachers and with one another, and the school commenced under the Spirit's control.[61]

These remarkable confessions were not just idle words, but rather a symptom of the repentance that had taken place deep within the heart, and subsequent actions proved the confessions had been real:

A doctor had boasted that he had one of the most honest cooks in Korea (in the East, cooks make all the purchases at the market); but when the cook was convicted he said, "I have been cheating the doctor all the time; my house and lot have been secured by cheating the doctor." The cook sold his home and paid all back to the doctor.

---

[61] (Goforth, 1943)

A deacon, who was looked upon as almost perfect, seemed to get very uneasy as the revival progressed, and he confessed to the stealing of some charity funds. All were astonished, but expected him to get peace; however, he descended into deeper distress and then confessed to a breach of the seventh commandment [adultery].

A woman, who for days seemed to pass through the agonies of hell, confessed one evening in a public meeting to the sin of adultery. The missionary in charge of the meeting was greatly alarmed, for he knew that her husband was present,[62] and knew that if that husband killed her he would be in accord with the Korean law. That husband in tears, went over and knelt beside his sinning wife and forgave her. How the Lord Jesus was glorified as He

---

[62] Though the Bible conference in Pyongyang had been men only due to space constraints at the meeting location, typical meetings had men and women gathering together.

said to that Korean woman, "Sin no more!"

Such extraordinary happenings could not but move the multitude, and the churches became crowded. Many came to mock, but in fear began to pray. The leader of a robber band, who came out of idle curiosity, was convicted and converted, and went straight to the magistrate and gave himself up. The astonished official said, "You have no accuser; you accuse yourself; we have no law in Korea to meet your case;" and so dismissed him.[63]

Public confession would be an ill-advised method to attempt to create a revival if used without the prerequisite of conviction, but there is no question of the powerful role it played in the Pyongyang Revival as a result of the conviction which fell upon believers and unbelievers alike.

---

[63] (Goforth, 1943)

As an expression of humility, repentance and obedience to the Word of God, these public confessions served a necessary purpose towards the continued work of the Spirit in the Pyongyang Revival.

The work of conviction in this revival seems to have come as a result of prayer, but only through the voluntary yielding to confession and repentance was the revival able to continue in power, as we have seen from these accounts above. The insight of the holiness of God, and the absolutely wicked nature of man was enough to bring great conviction to those in the revival meetings, but it was the testimony of changed lives of those who repented that drew others into the meetings to find out for themselves what kind of power could have impelled such fallen people to repent and be healed.

The level of conviction seen in the Pyongyang Revival may not be a common experience of believers, and physical falling-to-the-ground expression of conviction may be omitted from most church meetings today, but the Holy Spirit still speaks with His still small voice, and still only comes to those willing to respond in obedience. As preparation for revival, voluntary obedience to the Spirit's leading is critical—and conviction, confession and repentance on a small or large scale both prepare a person for service, as well as provide a testimony to onlookers of a life changed by the power of the Spirit.

May we be encouraged, like those in Zerubbabel's day, not to despise the small things (Zec 4:10), and not to quench the Spirit (1 Thess 5:19) whenever He appears, whether He comes in quietness or comes with intense expressions of conviction as seen in the Pyongyang Revival.

Conclusion

And precisely so far as our own land approximates to heathenism, it is impossible for God or man to promote religion in such a state of things but by powerful excitements. This is evident from the fact that this has always been the way in which God has done it. God does not create these excitements, and choose this method to promote religion for nothing or without reason.

   - Charles Finney, 1835 [64]

The stirring first-hand accounts of the Pyongyang Revival are interesting reading to be sure, but is there hope for a return of the Spirit in power in a similar way today? Could we dare to pray in expectation of the Lord to show favor upon us, and send His mighty Spirit to again perform an awesome work in our current environment?

---

[64] (Finney, 1835)

The missionaries in Korea were quite clear what was drawing the people to Christ in such conviction, as they reported:

> We knew that this eager, anxious throng were there because Jesus of Nazareth was passing by. At every service Christians came to the missionaries bringing those who had made their decision for Christ; from one or two to whole families. Idols were cast away and Christ was chosen. We could hear the Master's stately steppings and we felt that the place whereon we stood was holy ground.[65]

Are we looking for, even entreating, Jesus of Nazareth to pass by us, or are we hoping to bring the powerful excitements that Finney speaks about into our circle of influence by updated methods, beautiful buildings, and contemporary preaching?

---

[65] (Underwood, 1908)

Jonathan Goforth, author of one of the accounts heavily quoted above, diagnosed the issue quite clearly: "The Almighty Spirit is as willing to let Christ Jesus see of the travail of His soul in Canada and the United States as in Korea, but He does not get the yielded channels."[66]

Goforth explains:

> Surely God the Holy Spirit glorified our ascended Lord in Korea as certainly as He did in Palestine in the first century. It is a challenge to our easy-going Christianity to awake and seek God as these children of the East have done. They have given ample proof that it is not by might, nor by power, that the kingdom of God is made manifest among men. In all humility they yielded themselves to the Lord Jesus Christ, and the very fullness of God flowed through them. God waits to visit us with

---

[66] (Goforth, 1943)

the same fullness of salvation. But we must pay the price or merely have a name to live and be open to the condemnation of those who despise the Giver of so great salvation.[67]

Are you willing to live your life yielded to the Holy Spirit? To obey His leadings? Not to quench His promptings out of pride, self-consciousness, or self-concern? May we give the Holy Spirit empty vessels for Him to fill. May we not be so caught up with our own concerns that we neglect the God-breathed Scripture, but instead restore it to its rightful place of respect. May we be willing to come to our Lord Jesus in great desperation, with confidence in His unchanging character which enables us to ask for the wind of His Spirit to blow afresh among us today. May we have single-minded focus which clears away division and replaces personal concern with concern for His

---

[67] (Goforth, 1943)

Kingdom. And may we have the weighty gift of repentance—terrible to experience, but sweet to the soul on the other side of confession.

When a people can join together in such a condition—no longer hopeful in external circumstances, man-made methods, or satisfied with current results, but rather wholly dependent on seeing the Lord in His mighty power—then they can be sure the Lord will hear and answer from heaven, and respond as only our King can respond, with divine fire, grace and blessings so liberal that only He could ever afford such a powerful response.

He showed Himself strong in Pyongyang, Korea in 1907, and our God "is the same yesterday and today, yes and forever" (Heb 13:8).

Bibliography

Blair, W. N., & Hunt, B. F. (1977). *The Korean Pentecost and The Sufferings Which Followed*. Edinburgh: The Banner of Truth Trust.

Davis, G. T. (1910). *Korea for Christ*. New York: Fleming H. Revell Company.

Federal Council of Protestant Evangelical Missions in Korea. (1907). *Korea Mission Field*. Han'guk Kidokkyosa Yŏn'guhoe.

Finney, C. G. (1835). *Lectures on Revivals of Religion*. New York: Leavitt, Lord, & Co.

Goforth, J. (1943). *When the Spirit's Fire Swept Korea*. Grand Rapids: Zondervan.

Lee, G. (1907, March). How the Spirit came to Pyeng Yang. *The Chinese Recorder and Missionary Journal: Volume 38*, pp. 172-176.

Moffett, S. H. (1985). Where's the Power? *The Princeton Seminary Bulletin*, p. 59-67.

Underwood, L. H. (1908). *Fifteen Years Among the Top-knots, Or, Life in Korea.* American Tract Society.

Revival in India by Helen S. Dyer

(published 1907)

The Khassia Hills

"They have seen thy goings, O God; even the goings of my God, my King, in the sanctuary." – Psalm 68:24

According to the laws of the Spiritual Kingdom it was quite in order that the Welsh Revival should be reproduced on the Welsh corner of the Indian Mission Field.

These Welsh churches, called "Calvanistic Methodist," are conducted in Presbyterian order. The first droppings fell on a Presbytery of the Pariong district. The pastor of the churches of Ranthong (some miles away from a resident missionary) says: "I am very pleased to tell you that my Lord, who is full of mercy, has caused some showers of blessings to fall on this district. For ten days before the Pariong Presbytery, we had daily prayer meetings to ask God to send His Holy Spirit on us in that Presbytery. We felt that God was very near to us, and had a strong hope of seeing something wonderful, so went in good numbers, both men and women. We were not disappointed, for we saw with our own eyes in very truth the Holy Spirit descending with power on the people assembled there. Never had we experienced such a thing before, and we praise God for it...

To download and read the rest of this story, visit:

https://danielmweaver.com/

northkoreankeystorevival